How to Analyze People

The Ultimate Guide to Analyzing Others Instantly through Body Language, Psychological Techniques, Social Queues, and Human Behavior

Table of Contents

Introduction

Congratulations on purchasing your very own copy of *How to Analyze People*. Thank you so much for doing so!

The following chapters will discuss a subject that many people wish they were better at, and that is reading other people! The human race is naturally complex in nature, but thanks to many studies, heightening intelligence and basic know-how, there are proven ways to be able to analyze those around you in your everyday life.

You will discover how important it is to have this life skill and how it will benefit you in much more than the short term. We all have one thing in common, which is the wanted capability to step into the shoes of another to sincerely get to know them and find out what they are who they are and why individuals do the things they do!

As you venture through the chapters of this book, you will gain knowledge about various personality types that drive people in life, how people communicate with one another, how to utilize social and verbal cues to find out what you need to know about others, and much more! There is always a plus in honing the skill of getting to know people more than just skin deep. Good luck as you journey your way into human behavior!

There are plenty of books in regards to becoming better on reading people that are out there on the market, so thanks again for choosing this one! Every effort was made to ensure it is full of as much useful information as possible. Please enjoy!

Chapter 1
The Benefits of Learning Analyzing Techniques

When it comes to learning about the people around you more so than what they are wearing or seemingly coming off to you as there is a lot more to be said than what lies merely skin deep. Human beings are complicated creatures. We all have our own experiences and personalities that make us into who we are as individuals. It is one of the many things that make each and every single one of us unique! The chapters of this book will cover many ways to read people through the means of social cues, nonverbal language, and verbal techniques. But before we dive into all that vital information, it is good to know some of the benefits you will be receiving from absorbing the knowledge in this book as you become an excellent analyzer of the human race!

Connection with Others on Various Levels

The majority of the language we speak is not through our mouths at all, it is both consciously and unconsciously through our body language. Many of us tend to go through life pondering what to say to others, what not to say and just how to say it. Acquiring the knowledge of reading body language and other nonverbal communications is essential to truly connecting with those in your personal life, in the workplace and in other public settings. It allows you to not only better understand people but to expand your abilities in communicating as well. Picking up on the smallest of gestures can help you to become more understanding of others and inevitably leads you to be a much better communicator.

Double Your Business

If you are a business person or an entrepreneur, the reading of body language is crucial. Being able to recognize and become adaptable to the ways of a variety of people's body languages has the potential to make or break your business. For example, if you are meeting with a client and you continuously ramble on about your pitch, you may notice that their arms become crossed, as well as the interlocking of ankles with their torso facing away from you. Even though you thought you did a great job pitching your idea, the client turns down your deal. Learning to really understand body language can help you to notice signs during sales communications. If you take the time to notice the tiniest of nonverbal cues it may save many sales deals with potential customers! This can line your pockets more richly.

Prevention of Conflict

There are other kinds of nonverbal cues and body language we utilize, both consciously and unconsciously when we are upset or angry about something. It is important to acquire the knowledge needed to recognize defensive body language and nonverbal angry cues. This assists in a variety of situations, especially in close-bonded relationships. You can scale back the anger if you take the time to perform the right steps of action when you realize a person is upset with you. You can prevent unnecessary conflict from escalating. This is a win-win, for you can put an end to fighting and negative commentary that will only end up tarnishing relationships.

Improvement of Self-Presence

As you learn more and more about the body language and nonverbal cues of others, you will also start to take more notice as to the body language and other nonverbal signals you portray to those around you and in your life. Learning about this subject can help you become much more aware of your own body. Body language not only informs others what we are thinking and feeling, but it also influences how we feel overall as well. If you feel a bit down on yourself or about life in general, get up off the couch, stand tall and expand your chest. Performing this action just for a few minutes can help you regain that welcomed energy back into your body and mind, and create a feeling of self-confidence. Improving your own body language has an impact of positivity on yourself as well as those who are in your life!

Opens Up More Doors to the World

In the midst of body language, in just a mere half an hour, one person can transmit over 800 nonverbal signals to another person. By learning the ways of nonverbal communications, you can also teach your brain how to always know what to look for. In this, you may be surprised at what you actually begin seeing in the world that surrounds you. There have been many body language experts that have said learning the ways of nonverbal communication is like viewing the entirety of the world in high definition. You will be able to see a whole new layer of information that leads to a higher meaning of explanation.

Better Understanding of an Audience

As a public speaker, you are not going to prepare a speech for high school students that is meant for college students. The more you understand the background of the majority of your audience, the more you will be able to reach out to them as you tend to their personal needs. This will help you to prepare a speech that reaches out to the audience, instead of boring them. This is where analyzing people can be a make or break situation. Taking the time to examine the audience in which you will be speaking with will help you to uncover loads of new information that you can utilize to build a common foundation between you and the people you are speaking to.

Better in a Variety of Social Situations

We have all been in situations where we felt more than mildly uncomfortable, perhaps a flashback to your first high school or college party? We have no idea who the people are in certain scenarios, and we tend to stick to the sides of our close friends and people we know. As we grow older, however, this doesn't quite do the trick anymore. Unless you are lucky, you will not work with your best friends that you grew up with. You will have to venture into an entirely new realm of possibilities, including getting to know new people in such ways that will assist you in paving the path towards a continuously better career. In order to move up the food chain, it is vital to break out of our comfort zones and get to know new people. But people are not going to be receptive to you if you constantly appear uncomfortable, upset or unresponsive. Learning body language allows you to get a few steps ahead. While it teaches you how to read others, it also makes you privy to the aura you might be sending to others as well, leaving you to notice room for improvements. This goes for all types of social situations, even outside the workplace. The dating world is modernly vast thanks to technology and cellular applications. We can now meet people via tech screens, which leads to more potential issues. The first time people meet, it can be naturally awkward. But you can avoid some of these feelings between you and the other person by becoming consciously aware of their cues as well as the way you are portraying yourself.

Chapter 2
Becoming Educated on Human Personality Types

In order to really get to know other people, you must be privy and become educated to the fact that there are quite a few personality types in regards to the human race, as well as temperaments. While life experiences and lessons help create us into who we are, for we are born hardwired with personality types that fuel the things we do and provide insight to our actions, speech, futures, etc. As an analyzer, I assure you that you will find this chapter not only intriguing but quite useful when it comes to acquiring the knowledge packed within the remaining chapters of this book. So let's dive in, shall we?

Personality Types

The Fulfiller of Duty

Genuine and tranquil, these people are intrigued by security and serene living. To a great degree,they are intensive, mindful, and true. They are very creative when it to focusing. Generally intrigued by supporting and advancing conventions and foundations, these individuals are efficient and persevering, working consistently towards recognized objectives. They can more often than not finish any assignment once they have decided to do it.

The Mechanic

Peaceful and reserved in nature, these people are intrigued by how and why things function. They tend to have phenomenal abilities with mechanical things. They are daring individuals who they live for the occasion and are generally inspired by and capable at extreme sports. These individuals are quite uncomplicated in their wishes and are faithful to their associates and to their inside esteem frameworks, however, they are not excessively worried about regarding laws and tenets on the off chance that they impede completing something. Disengaged and expository, they exceed expectations at discovering answers for common sense issues.

The Nurturer

Tranquil, kind, and reliable, anyone can be relying on these people to get things completed in a timely, efficient and complete manner. These individuals are known to put the requirements of others over their own needs. Steady and with common sense, they esteem security and customs. All around created a feeling of space and capacity. They have a rich internal universe of perceptions about individuals and to a great degree, discerning of other's emotions, all the while being inspired by the serving of others.

The Artist

Calm, genuine, touchy and kind, these people do their best not to clash with others, and not liable to do things which may produce strife, making them steadfast and dependable. To a great degree, they are very creative and tasteful, which leads them to gratefulness for excellence. Not keen on driving or controlling others, they are adaptable and liberal and are typically prone to be unique and innovative, which makes them appreciate the present moment.

The Protector

Unobtrusively mighty, unique, and delicate, these individuals tend to stick to things until the point when they are finished. Because of this, they are intuitive to such a degree that they are worried about their own sentiments just as much as they are about the feelings, needs and wants of others. They create self-esteem frameworks which they entirely stick to. They are well known for their perseverance in making the best choice, which makes them liable to be individualistic, as opposed to driving or following.

The Idealist

Peaceful, intelligent, and optimistic in nature, these people are keen on serving mankind. They have well-established systems of value, which they live strongly by which makes them amazingly steadfast, versatile and laid-back unless a firmly held esteem is undermined. Normally, capable essayists, they are rationally speedy and ready to see potential outcomes, making them very keen on comprehension and assisting others.

The Scientist

Autonomous, unique and expository in nature, these people have an outstanding capacity to transform speculations into action. They are highly knowledgeable in creating strong plans of action, which leaves them to successfully get significance from their dreams and makes them long-term masterminds. They are known to have elevated requirements for their execution, and the execution of others. They are natural born leaders, however, will take after another on the off chance that they know and can trust to follow them.

The Thinker

Coherent, unique, innovative masterminds, these people can turn out to be exceptionally excited for speculations and thoughts. Extraordinarily competent and headed to transform speculations into clear understandings. They are skilled and rational, which makes them calm and reserved, which may make them hard to become more well acquainted with. They are individualistic, having no enthusiasm for driving or tailing others.

The Doer

Well disposed, versatile, activity situated, these people are "Practitioners" who are centered on quick outcomes. They live for the here and now, which makes them daring individuals who live quick paced ways of life. Restless with long clarifications, they place a great degree of faith in those they know and trust, yet not normally deferential of laws and tenets on the off chance that they impede completing things. These individuals are great at building incredible relationships due to their people skills and abilities.

The Guardian

Down to earth, conventional, and organized in nature, these people are prone to be athletic. Not intrigued by hypothesis or deliberation unless they see the down to earth application, they have clear dreams of the way things ought to be. Steadfast and persevering, they typically like to be in control. These individuals are usually good citizens who take great value in security and tranquil living.

The Performer

These individuals are typically arranged and carefree, they make things more fun for others by their delight. Living for the occasion, they cherish new encounters. They hate hypothesis and generic examination. Inspired by serving others, they are liable to be the focal point of consideration in social circumstances. They have a good development of common sense that makes them very practical people.

The Caregiver

Cordial, well known, and principled these people tend to put the necessities of others over their own needs. They feel a solid awareness of other's expectations and obligations, making them highly value traditions and the value of security, which makes them intrigued by serving others. Need uplifting feedback to create a good sense of self-worth and they have a well-created sense of functionality and space.

The Inspirer

Energetic, hopeful, and inventive, these people are ready to do nearly anything that interests them. They inhabit incredible relationship building abilities. They have a desirable need to live within the means of their inner values and are energized by new thoughts, however, exhausted with points of interest. These people are open-minded and able to adapt well, with a wide scope of interests and capabilities under their belt.

The Giver

Well known and touchy, with remarkable relationship building abilities, these people are almost always remotely engaged, with genuine worry of how others think and feel. They normally detest being separated from everyone else. They see everything from the human point and typically dislike impersonal analysis. Exceptionally powerful at overseeing individual's issues, and driving gathering discourses, they are inspired by serving others, and presumably put the necessities of others over their own particular needs.

The Visionary

Innovative, clever, and mentally speedy, these people are great at a wide scope of things. They highly appreciate debating issues, and might be into "one-upmanship". They get exceptionally thrilled for new thoughts and activities, yet may disregard the more standard parts of life. They tend to be straightforward and emphatic and appreciate individuals and are quite the stimulant company. They are equipped with the phenomenal capacity to comprehend ideas and apply rationale to discover arrangements.

The Executive

Self-assured and candid, these people are driven to be leaders. They tend to have an incredible capacity to comprehend troublesome authoritative issues and make strong arrangements. Clever and very much educated, they, as a rule, exceed expectations at public speaking. They highly value learning and acquiring new skills, and for the most part have little tolerance with wastefulness or disorganization.

Human Temperaments

While there are a broad variety of personality types to fit into a wide array of people, there are actually four types of temperaments that stem from the personality types you just read about. Where do these temperaments stem from exactly? Ironically, directly from humorism! Humor in this instance reflects on how our bodily fluids are present within us. Each person has slightly different proportions of these fluids than the next, and the predominance of one fluid over another defines our temperament. The dominance of one humor is stated to affect the behavior and appearance of a person. Many people have a decent mixture of temperaments, so it may be difficult to decipher who is what. While the concept of the four temperaments theory is typically dismissed by many in modern medicine and psychology, it is still a fun little thing to learn about and keep in mind when analyzing human behavior as a whole!

Sanguine Personality Type

Individuals with this personality type have a tendency to be energetic, idealistic, light, and lighthearted. They adore enterprise and have a high hazard resistance. Commonly, Sanguine individuals are exceptionally poor at enduring fatigue and will look for more variety and amusement. Obviously, this quality may some of the time adversely influence their sentimental connections. Since this disposition is inclined to delight looking for practices, many individuals with this personality type are probably going to battle with addictions. Their steady desires may prompt indulging and weight issues. These individuals are exceptionally inventive and may wind up being incredible specialists. Moreover, they are awesome performers and will normally do well on the off chance that they pick professions in a media outlet. They typically have more natural abilities in the following areas when it comes to jobs:

- Sports

- Cooking

- Fashion

- Travel

- Marketing

Phlegmatic Personality Type

Somebody with this personality type tends to be indifferent and generally is social butterflies. They look for relational amicability and cozy connections. These individuals are faithful life partners and cherishing guardians. They save their associations with old companions, inaccessible relatives, and neighbors. Individuals with this personality have a tendency to evade clashes and dependably attempt to intervene between others to reestablish peace and amicability. They are particularly into charity and helping other people. The ideal careers for those with phlegmatic personality are:

- Social services

- Child development

- Psychology

- Counseling

- Teaching

- Nursing

Choleric Personality Type

Somebody with this personality type has the potential to be unadulterated and irritable but is goal oriented. Individuals with this identity are extremely sagacious, explanatory, and sensible. To a great degree, commonsense and clear, these individuals aren't fundamental or great allies or especially social. They loathe casual chitchat and appreciate profound and important discussions. They would preferably be distant from everyone else than in organization of shallow individuals. In short, they need to invest energy with individuals who have comparable expert premiums. The ideal jobs for those who fall into the choleric personality type are:

- Business

- Programming

- Engineering

- Statistics

- Technology

- Management

Melancholic Personality Type

Individuals with this personality type really love traditions and everything about them. Ladies cook for men; men open entryways for ladies. They cherish their families and companions and, dissimilar to cheerful personality, they don't search for oddity and enterprise. Truth be told, they stay away from it no matter what. Somebody with this personality type is probably not going to wed a non-native or leave their country for another nation. They are extremely social and look to add to the group. Being to a great degree deliberate and precise, these individuals are fabulous managers of other people. The ideal career options for those with melancholic personality are:

- Administration

- Social work

- Accounting

- Management

Chapter 3
How to Analyze People's Personalities

Now that you have become educated about the various types of personalities among the human population, it is time to discover some different methods in analyzing the personalities of people you know as well as strangers you come across. There is not necessarily a formula for understanding people, but there are some basic and good to know techniques to have you mentally equipped in case you ever need to utilize them. While personality can be moderately distinguished based upon body language and facial features or a person's actions, truly analyzing the personality of an individual requires one to have a deeper know-how of many other aspects than just nonverbal communication.

How to Analyze Personality

I enjoy using examples when it comes to illustrating something complicated concepts. So for you to truly grasp the idea of analyzing people's personalities, I will lead you through the information in this chapter by means of an example I use when teaching many people about this skill.

I met Bob the first time at the gym. We never really spoke to one another but I took notice over time that he came in during the same time period each day. While a seemingly unimportant detail, but to me as an analyzer, it showed me that Bob was a self-motivator who did not like to procrastinate. I also gathered the traits of being strong-willed and organized mentally and that he always seemed to have a sense of urgency when it came to how he spent his time at the gym. All of these traits were visible to me just by his punctuality to showing up at the gym.

Another aspect of Bob I noticed was what he wore to the gym. He always wore workout clothing that revealed his muscles. He was also one of the only ones to perform intriguing exercises, which told me his need for attention and wanting to be showy. During a conversation at the gym, later on, I discovered that Bob was an only child. When it comes to analyzing the personality of another person, one must find the importance of the birth order of an individual. Bob, being an only child, was more than likely given lots of attention during their childhood which made the "center of attention" attitude at the gym makes more sense.

Bob also almost always wore black clothing, even when he changed out of his workout clothing he put on black clothes. One day I noticed his mobile device and not to my surprise, it was protected by a black phone case as well. When analyzing people, you may find that some go to one extreme to the other when they are attempting to get away from something. Coming into a gym wearing black gave me the impression that Bob wanted to come off as tough in nature, maybe even dangerous. Like the "bad boy" type of guy.

After another conversation with Bob, I found that my other expectations ringed true. He was bullied growing up, which made him feel weak. Growing up, he did his absolute best to hide that past by going to the gym, appearing tough and wearing black.

Another rule of thumb when it comes to analyzing individuals is that as you connect the dots to someone's personality, they should always lead you to a type of straight line. If my assumptions of Bob "wanting to be powerful" were true, then we would need to expect that he would be performing and conducting in other actions that would assist him in becoming more powerful, other than going to the gym. With another conversation, I found my answer. Bob was interested in martial arts. People tend to be interested in things that help them move towards an important goal of theirs, and away from the identity that they hate.

How to Get to Know Someone's Personality

There are many factors as we dive into the nitty-gritty of getting to truly know the personality of another human being. From body language, preferences in color and the choices one makes, these are just a few of the main factors that can lead us to gather the necessary information into the personality traits of a person. There is no "perfect map" into getting the picture right 100%, but knowing some of the inner workings can indeed help you to analyze another person's personality.

To truly understand the personal characteristics of another human being, you must become seasoned in a bit of psychology. The behaviors of a person may seem either totally odd or completely meaningless when seen by itself, but it can be of great significance when it all comes together with the remaining actions a person does.

For example, someone who spends half of their money to purchase a fancy car might seem very irrational and unwise, but when taking the time to connect the dots a bit, you may find that they have a love for being the center of attention, so it becomes apparent why they made that decision. In saying this, in order to get a good perspective into someone's personality, you must put judgment to the side. Just because a particular action seemed irrational does not mean there is no other explanation.

Putting Together the Past with Personality

To really get aspects of a person's true personality accurate, you must get to know a little about them and their past. How did this individual grow up? How were they treated as a child? What were their relationships like with parents and siblings? For example, you will see that the youngest sibling in the family may become extremely ambitious as a result of being the weakest kid. They feed off ambition because this makes them feel more powerful or as powerful as the oldest sibling. After knowing such a tiny fact, many other things become clearer, such as why this particular person may want to become a millionaire, etc. This does not mean that every young kid will grow up to have an ambitious side, however. This is just a prime example to prove that knowing a bit about someone's past can be a precursor to their actions in the now.

Personality and Dreams

While many people are hesitant to speak about their past, especially to new people, they are more open to talking about the dreams. Little do they know is, they are giving away a lot more about themselves in this manner than they would be speaking about all the occurrences in their past history. Pay attention to what people say about their dreams, hopes, and desires. It can be just the key you need to unlock a whole new doorway to their personality that you didn't know you would ever receive.

Ways to Know Personality through Social Media Posts

The world today would be seemingly obsolete to many without the utilization of technology and social networking. That being said, there is a lot to be said about what people post on their social media profiles that you can decipher and get many personality clues from.

In order to analyze someone's personality via the assistance of their social media, you will need a sample of posts. Moods change and vary all the time, which can make it difficult to form a good, solid conclusion about the individual whose posts you are looking at. You will have to do a bit of working connecting different posts together to find common things. While not all common posts should say the same thing, they should be pointing in a particular direction, in which then you can confidently come to a conclusion about that person via their posts. Also, photos and videos can share a wide variety of crucial information as well!

- **Constantly repeated words/phrases** – In a later chapter, you will learn more about the importance of the things that people say. Is there a word or phrase this person used consistently throughout their social media posts? These may reflect inner desires, wants, needs, beliefs and feelings. For example, if there are words such as "success, achieve, rich, goal, strive" repeated many times throughout time, this suggests that this individual may be a bit obsessed with success and wealth.

- **Do posts point out same or similar things?** – Jokes made about money, posts about celebrities, videos about expensive items can clearly point out that individual's desire to make more money.

- **Pictures that agree with posts** – If a person utilizes the word "independent" many times or "alone" excessively along with the use of many solo photos taken, you can easily come to a conclusion that this person relies on himself.

Chapter 4
Interpreting Body Language

We spend our lives figuring out how to decipher other individuals' nonverbal prompts. While we're caught up with attempting to unravel their messages, they are additionally attempting to disentangle our own. There are times when you need other individuals to know precisely how you're feeling, particularly when those sentiments are both positive and responded. This isn't generally simple to do, particularly in case you're not an especially emotive sort of individual. At different circumstances, in any case, you certainly need to conceal your inward sentiments. To keep away from passionate spillage, you may need to work doubly hard. Contingent upon the circumstance, you may need to put on your Lady Gaga-style poker face.

Nonverbal communication is quite literally the dialect of the body. You may surmise that you just demonstrate your feelings through your face, however, that is truly just the tip of the iceberg. Your whole body partakes in the matter of either appearing or concealing your mental state. To control that show implies you need to control your body's oblivious prompts. This guide will demonstrate to you how, starting from the top. When you're set, you'll have a substantially more prominent comprehension of seemingly insignificant bodily gestures that can give those that actually pay attention signals that give way to what someone might actually be thinking and feeling. We will work our way from the tippy-top of our heads all the way down to our toes!

The Head

When I said we were going to begin at the very top of the head, I meant just that! Your hair and scalp can tell others a lot about your mental and emotional state of mind. People have good and bad hair days, but sometimes that should not be overlooked so easily. When one is stressed, perhaps they forget to brush out their lovely locks. At a single glance, one may take notice that you may not be completely together at that moment. Or, having bed head may make one assume that you have a sexy night on the town the night before. No matter the cut, style or color of your hair, having a groomed appearance tells others that you are in control of the way your day is turning out. If you do not have hair, that problem may be solved but it also leaves your brows to question. They can give away cues such as excessive frowning which is a pretense as to how you might be feeling.

The other permanent features of your face cannot be changed (unless you go under the knife and receive plastic surgery!) but they can prominently display and give away cues as to what you are experiencing and going through to others. The smallest movements that our faces make can give away a lot of what we are thinking to others. These are known by psychologists as "micro-expressions." These are vital in truly interpreting body language because they can lead to a contradiction of what someone might be saying, which leads one to believe that what is coming out of someone's mouth might not be as truthful as it sounds. For example, if you are attracted to someone and wish to impress them, you may have those butterflies within you that you think you are hiding well. But the slightest pulling of the muscles in such areas like the mouth shows that you are panicking a bit on the inside. Take a moment to grimace for a second. Take note of how your entire face feels when you do so. There are many micro expressions that people protrude on the outside when they are afraid, lying, etc. If you wish to be dishonest for good reasons, learn how to control these facial muscles, for they will give you away quicker than your white lie will.

Your eyes are also a big source of nonverbal communication. When learning how to communicate with people more openly and thoroughly, you need to learn about the balance of looking and staring, for there is a fine line. Too much looking into someone else's eyes can cause discomfort in the other person, while too little can make you seem uninterested. This includes eye gestures such as eye rolls, etc. A twinkle of the eye can make others around you feel at ease, do not underestimate the power of a smirk or smile!

The chin and neck are not to be forgotten either! While they are both facial features we are born with and cannot change, if you are constantly jutting your chin out in front of you, people may read you and assume you're obstinate. The neck has the ability to be flexible and is not a fixed area of the body. But the way you hold your head up can say a lot about you as a person and also what you might be thinking or feeling at any certain time. If you choose to hold your head straight up, you will appear confident. If your eyes are always scanning the floor, the opposite will seem true.

The Torso

If you hold your neck up nice and straight, then your torso will follow this action and align right along with it. Confidence will show if you keep your shoulders and back straight and not hunching forward. If you rather choose to sag more around the torso, perhaps you are trying to gain the attention of someone who is sympathetic. Chronic sagging in the torso area tells others that you may not feel good physically or mentally or that you are very unconfident in yourself. Keeping yourself in a solid upright position has more good effects than non-verbally informing people you are confident in yourself. Always allowing your torso area of the body to sag will lead to a variety of pesky health problems later on. So sit up straight!

The Arms and Hands

Your upper limbs give way to perhaps the most essential and most easy to read tools of the human body when it comes to accurately reading body languages. They can nonverbally communicate a lot of things, including things you wish not to inform others around you of. Excessive hand fidgeting can portray boredom or anxiety. Tightly crossing your arms may make you seem like you are angry. Arrogant mannerisms like placing your arms akimbo may be unintentional but other people highly read into those sorts of mannerisms. It is important if you do not want to give yourself away *too* much that you learn to neutrally keep your hands and arms from giving away impressions that are actually not true to you. The most recommended way to keep your hands and arms is to hold them in your lap. When you are standing, keep them at your sides or in another resting place that is comfortable for you so that it does not look forced to other people.

The Legs

The lower limbs of your body give away just as much as your upper extremities do. If you tightly cross your legs this may create a "closed off" view to other people. But splaying them out makes you seem too carefree and careless. In order to create a comfortable, relaxed and open-minded feel to others you need to be relaxed but not so much so that it seems like you are bored with the situation at hand. What we wear can make differences in this, however. Obviously, women who wear skirts will have to keep their legs closed tighter than if they are wearing pants. This is why it is stressed to not wear too short of skirts or other clothing that makes you feel uncomfortable in your own skin. The anxiety of trying to look good in articles of clothing that you otherwise do not feel your best in *will* show to others.

Anxious feelings can also present themselves physically through the means of excessive leg shaking and foot tapping. People who come off jittery may just want to burn off a few excess calories, but more than likely they feel anxious about the situation around them or about something that may be on their mind. The legs make up the biggest part of the human body, so even with the smallest movements, people take notice. Instead of shaking your legs, be conscious of other ways you can prevent this. To help the bodily jitters, make it a habit, even in scenarios that aren't the most comfortable, to sit with your legs gently crossed and your hands nicely folded in your lap. Not only will other people take notice of how calm you seem, but it will help you to settle feelings of anxiousness as well.

The Feet

If you are someone that shakes their legs, then you inevitably are going to shake your feet simultaneously as well. There is also the tapping of toes, which can indicate to others that you might be in a rush or anxious to get going. Tapping of the feet also may be used to gain the attention of another person if you do not want to come off as rude if you say something. Toe tapping is typically a body language that is used when someone feels pressured for time and does not want to rudely engage in conversation, even if it would get the ball rolling faster. But in reality, these people may be seen as rude anyways or just plain annoying with all that tapping!

Did you know that your feet can also communicate to others of fearful feelings and confidence? It is all about the way you move from point A to point B. If you walk in a stride that is straight and strong, you come across as someone that people can depend on. Good posture of any sort portrays confidence to others. Slouching and slumping, however, portray a lack of confidence or ever a fear of where you might be going. You give off cues unconsciously by being either fearful or confident in your destination. Also, if someone wants or is interested in engaging with you, their feet will point right towards you. If their feet are pointing away from you, their minds are on another topic and it is a sign they would either rather be somewhere else or may be in a slight hurry and have another place to be at the time.

A Few Tricks in Reading Body Language

As you have read so far in this chapter, the ability to read the body language of others can give us a lot of information about those around us. If you feel like you will never be good at reading body language, chin up! We as human beings actually pick up on more bodily cues than we realize. Only 7% of communication comes from verbal speaking while 38% comes from just the tone in our voices and 55% comes from nonverbal body language. Learning to become aware of that much bigger percentage can give you an edge over others and even pave your way to success! So, next time you are in a meeting, on a date, having fun with your kids or hanging out with friends, watch for the following cues:

- **Crossed arms and legs** – This action portrays possible resistance to your ideas or the thoughts of others. The arms and legs are physical barricades that suggest that they may not be quite as open as to what you are saying, even if they happen to have a smile on their face and seem quite intrigued by what is spewing from your mouth. If someone's arms and legs are crossed, it is a pretty telling sign that they are blocked off from everything in front of them, mentally and emotionally. While it may not be intentional, it is still very revealing of the way they think and feel.

- **Smile with crinkled eyes** – When you view the smile of others, a smile can lie through anything, but the sparkle in the eye and the creases a true smile makes around the eyes can't. Smiles that are genuine reach all the way up to the eyes. People often smile to hide their feelings and thoughts. So the next time you see someone smile at you, do not take as much notice of their pearly whites, but rather the crinkles that are created by the smile at the corner of the eyes. If they are non-existent, they are using the smile as a shield to hide something.

- **The copying of your body language** – While this sounds like a child-like game, the mirroring of body language is how we tend to bond with people in an unconscious manner. In social environments as you engage, does that person cross their legs when you do? Do they cock their heads in the same way you do when conversing with others? The copying of body language is actually a sign that the conversation itself is going great and that the other people are being quite receptive to what you are saying. This is useful when it comes to negotiating, for it shows you actual proof that the opposing party is considering your deal.

- **Posture creates a story** – Think about a person of power in your life, whether in the workplace or elsewhere. Take note of their posture. More than likely these individuals will walk into a room with an erect posture, palms facing down and communicate nonverbally with open gestures. Posture is critical in providing a story to others about your life. Standing straight with shoulders back portrays a position of power. While slouching portrays less power. Maintaining a decent posture tells others that you command to be respected and promotes engagement to others, whether or not you are a leader.

- **Lying eyes** – I am sure most of you remember the phrase of "look at me in the eye when I am speaking to you." Growing up, we were taught that avoiding eye contact was a perfect sign of lying. But that is common knowledge, so many people lie to one another even while maintaining perfect eye contact. That is why those that are being dishonest tend to overcompensate eye contact, giving it to others to the point of discomfort. Seven to ten seconds is the average that people hold eye contact for, longer when they are listening rather than speaking. If you come into contact with someone whose eye contact makes you uncomfortable, especially someone who doesn't bother to blink, they are more than likely being dishonest with you.

- **Discomfort in the brows** – There are a few main emotions that our eyebrows portray: fear, worry, and surprise. It is impossible to have raised eyebrows and attempting to have a casual conversation. If you are talking about something that shouldn't be causing any eyebrows to raise, something else is going on around you or with that person internally.

- **Excessive nodding** – If you are speaking to someone and they are constantly nodding their head, this may signal that they are concerned about your thoughts or they may doubt your ability to follow through with something.

- **Clenched jaw** – Clenched jaws, tightening of the neck and a furrowed brow are all tell-tale signs of stress. It doesn't matter what is coming from a person's mouth, if any of these signs are noticeable, they are hiding their anxiety, stress, and discomfort. Perhaps a conversation is leading down a path of something they are not comfortable speaking about. They key here is to take note of any mismatches of what the person is saying and then what their body language is telling you.

This chapter does not only gave you as the reader a few tips on improving your self-image to others but also cues to look for when attempting to read another person's personality and mind. These will help you to know what another individual is feeling, especially if you choose to comfort them. Notice the way they either provide you with good or bad eye contact. Look down from time to time, are their feet facing you? There are tiny ways to diagnose body language and how one truly feels in various scenarios. Like every great skill, practice makes perfect. As you learn the once mysterious ways of body language, ask a friend or family member if you could practice reading their language. The body both consciously and unconsciously reflects the mental state we are in. As you learn and become more seasoned in reading people, you may start to notice things you can change to come off more calm and relaxed to others. This helps quite a bit in the world of dating. You do not want a stranger on a first date to feel on edge because you seem on edge physically. Learning to control your bodily cues in social environments is key to many things, including getting a step or two ahead in this dog-eat-dog world. While it is not yet possible to actually read a person's exact thoughts, you can learn a lot if not just enough from nonverbal body language.

Chapter 5
Learning to Read People by How They Speak

Now that you learned about some body language and nonverbal cues, it is time to talk about and take into account the things that we verbally say. The words people say can be a tell-tale sign of their personalities. Even single phrases said by another can tell others truckloads about their desires, personal needs and wants. But the important part of analyzing people through their verbal speech is learning what they may be trying to cover up and hide from the rest of the world. Each and everything that a person says tends to reveal at least something that makes up their personality. The actions, beliefs, and thoughts of individuals all make up the aspects of who we are as human beings. All the things people do or think can uncover lots of information about their personality, as well as what makes them up psychologically.

How Words Uncover Personalities

Our perception of the world and other individuals is created through our concerns of other people. For example, *"Hey, did you grow shorter overnight?"* seems like a joke, right? Well, in the context said it probably was, but when you examine simple phrases like this, there is a whole lot more that is actually being said. Even though the person who stated this joke was more than likely just kidding, it shows that they might be uncomfortable with their own physical height. It is not by the phrase he communicated that gave away his concerns about his height, but rather that we were wearing a different sort of shoe when he said it to his buddy. This individual may also be weary of his appearance physically as well and may even be carrying around a low self-confidence because of their insecurity about their looks. While in this example there may be many other different factors that play along with why this phrase was said, this is just a small yet prime example that we should be learning to read "between the lines" of what people are telling us.

How Words Uncover Insecurities

For this section, we shall utilize a different example. Imagine two people at the gym, lifting weights. They do not know one another but are standing side by side while exercising. A third individual comes in and says "You both are standing too close to one another, take care so you don't get hurt!" The distance between the two lifting weights was not close enough to end up in a gym tragedy, so the fact that the third person went out of their way to tell the two gym-goers this was because they viewed the situation much more dangerous than it actually way. This gives a clue to the personality type of the third person, more than likely they are someone who worries a lot and their perception of the world around them is then exaggerated by the probability of negativity that whirls around their mind a lot of the time. That third person more than likely becomes fearful of major issues that ever arise in their life because of this excessive worrying.

The Things We Say = Doorway in Who We Are

Even the smallest of things people say are indicators of who they are as an individual. The things we say communicate what we need as well as insecurities and other personality defects we may have, even if they are not directly communicated as such or if we had different intentions when we speak them. Many people tell jokes all the times without taking into account that the words they are spewing from their mouths can reveal much more than they intended in regards to their true personality. Anyone that is a good analyzer will pick up on the smallest of verbal cues to assess them.

Word Clues

If the eyes are the window to the spirit, at that point words are the portal to the brain. Words speak to thoughts. To understand someone else's musings is to tune into the words what he or she talks or composes. Certain words mirror the behavioral attributes of the individual who talked or kept in touch with them. These are known as word clues. Word clues increment the likelihood of anticipating the behavioral qualities of people by investigating the words they pick when they talk or write. Word clues alone can't decide the traits of someone's personality, yet they do give bits of knowledge into the manner of thinking and behavioral qualities. Speculations can be created in view of word clues and afterward tried by utilizing extra data evoked from the individual or outsider confirmation.

The human mind is unbelievably proficient. When we think, we utilize just verbs and nouns. Descriptors, intensifiers, and different parts of speech are included amid the change of contemplations into talked or composed language. The words we include reflect our identity and what we are considering.

All proper sentence structures utilize both a very and a noun. For example, let's look at this simplistic sentence" "I walked." Short and sweet, it still consists of the pronoun "I" and the verb the subject is doing, "walked". Any other words put into this simple sentence are modifications of the quality of the noun or the action in which the noun is taking. Their modifications are made deliberately, which provide analyzers clues as to the personality of the person speaking, as well as behavioral characteristics of the speaker or writer.

Word clues enable spectators to create theories or make instructed surmises in regards to the behavioral attributes of others. For instance, in the sentence "I immediately strolled," the Word clue "immediately" creates a feeling of urgency, however, it didn't give the motivation to the desperation. Someone may "rapidly walk" since they might be late for an arrangement or expects to be late for an arrangement. Upright individuals consider themselves to be dependable and don't have any desire to be late for arrangements. Individuals who need to be on time tend to regard social standards and need to satisfy the desires of others. Individuals with this behavioral trademark make great representatives since they would prefer not to frustrate their bosses. Individuals "rapidly walk" when they experience general dangers. A general danger may happen while strolling through an awful neighborhood. Moving toward awful climate could likewise display a risk. Strolling rapidly to stay away from an electrical storm lessens the risk of a lightning strike or getting wet. Individuals may include "rapidly" for an assortment of reasons, however, there is a particular explanation behind their decision.

Word clues show a noninvasive strategy to adequately read individuals without their knowledge. The following examples will show how word clues give bits of knowledge into the behavioral attributes of individuals when they talk or write.

- *"I won another award."* – The word clue "another" is a sign that the speaker of this sentence has won previous awards. By telling it in this manner, they wanted others to know that they have at least one other award, otherwise bumping up their image of self. They may desire and need praise from others to reinforce their self-esteem and overall confidence. Analyzers could see this as a vulnerability by the use of flattery and other comments that could enhance that individual's ego.

- *"I worked hard to achieve my goal."* – The word clue "hard" portrays that the person who said this phrase values things that are difficult to reach or achieve. In saying this, it gives away that the goal they are speaking about is harder than goals that they typically attempt to take on. "Hard" also gives away that this individual put off the need for gratification and believes that hard work and dedication will end with great results. Potential employees with these types of characteristics would more than likely accept challenges thrown their way with determination and would be successful at completing those tasks thoroughly.

- *"I patiently sat through the lecture."* – The word clue "patiently" can give away several things. It could mean that the individual was quite bored with the lecture itself. Maybe they had to return a phone call that was important at the time. Maybe they needed to use the bathroom. No matter the reasoning behind what this person said, they were obviously focused on something else other than the lecture at hand. People who wait for a break before leaving to use the restroom adhere to social norms. Those who receive calls get up and leave the room more than likely do not follow social boundaries as well. People who abide consistently by social boundaries can be seen as great employees because they tend to respect authority. On the other hand, those who do not quite adhere to social boundaries are better suited for jobs that require them to think in novel manners.

- *"I decided to buy that model."* – The word clue "decided" signifies that the person who said this sentence weighed a few options before making a purchase. It shows that they may have struggled a bit in making a final decision. This behavior indicates that this person tends to think things through thoroughly before acting. "Decided" also may show that this individual is usually not impulsive in nature. One who is more impulsive would probably say something more along the lines of *"I just bought that model."* The word clue "just" suggest that this individual purchased the item without much thought at all.

- *"I did the right thing."* – The word clue "right" gives away that the person who said this sentence has struggled with ethical dilemmas recently or in the past and has overcome them. This trait says that this individual has great strength when it comes to their character and tends to make the right decision, even when opposing views may be thrown their way.

Reading the Minds of People through Their Words

Repetition of Particular Words

"That car is powerful."

"This color is strong."

"I do not have the strength to study."

If you are to look at those three sentences above at first glance, you probably would not get many clues from them. But analyzers learn how to look at the things people say a bit closer. Notice the words "power", "strong", and "strength". All of them mean powerful. The distribution of the words in our minds does not happen randomly, but rather with the words we say are typically in reference to our concerns, desires, and needs. The person who said the phrases above is concerned about strength, power and being weak. He probably wants to be strong or he thinks he needs to be stronger or he might be concerned about becoming powerful.

The Telling of Stories

"I was strolling with my two friends yesterday and a big man appeared suddenly out of nowhere. We all thought he was coming towards us to pick a fight but at the last second he looked away and walked past us."

What is there to say from this little story? It was actually stated by the same individual from above that was concerned with power. The word "big man" is a reflection of this person's desire to be strong either emotionally or physically. But any person would have told the story the same way, right? No. This person stated is like this, and even though the man walked away from them, he still used the word clues "big man" in the sentence. This is obviously what he was concerned with the most at that time.

Hidden Messages within Jokes

'There are kids sitting at a table in a restaurant. When the waiter comes to take their order, one of the kids says, *"I will have anything that costs one million dollars!"'*

Obviously, this kid was joking. But as you have learned thus far, there are a lot of vital clues regarding that individual in everything they say. This kids' concern with money is pretty definite in this joke. He more than likely has grown up in a family with parents that have taught them that money is important. Or they may have suffered financially due to poor resources, etc.

Chapter 6
How to Become an Expert Profiler

In order to analyze people in a thorough, concise manner, one must learn the psychology of why people act the way they do and becoming seasoned with profiling people can help you to master this ability. It is important to pause the world around you and take the time to observe the actions and words of other people. While travel is meant to get to Point A to Point B, have you ever stopped to look further into the details of the hustle and bustle of an average traveler? In order to analyze people, you must be willing to see *beyond* what see!

The Basics of Profiling

Viewing People as Onions

While this may sound funny, a person's entire being should be visualized like the four layers of an onion. The deeper you get into the onion, the more you are able to determine how much you can really read into someone.

- *Skin* – Without being consciously aware of it, we tend to reveal more about ourselves to other people than we realize through personalities and traits.

- *Second layer* – This layer is often seen by people we have gotten to know better and who we appreciate in our lives, like co-workers and classmates. Since there is a sense of comfort and trust built between, people are able to comprehend one another on a basic level here.

- *Third layer* – This is a layer seen by best friends and other people we form close bonds with. There is a "locked" sense of trust and security with people that know you at this layer. We share secrets, pronounce concerns and other similar things.

- *Core* – Each and every person as a core. This is where secrets and thoughts are stored that are not shared with anyone but oneself. This layer is quite psychological.

Elimination of Barriers and Personal Prejudice

In order to really analyze others, you must be willing to tear down the barriers that you think are the truth about yourself and others. You must at times force yourself to believe and come to conclusions that you otherwise would not have. We have whisked away into scenarios that leave us feeling guilty and insecure, which blinds us into accepting the reality of things. Prejudice in the world of psychology goes way beyond just race and gender. You must acknowledge that prejudice is all about basing thoughts and opinions on ideas without facts. It is crucial to keep yourself in a neutral state of mind before getting consumed by false statements.

Test on Someone You Already Know

It is important when you are just beginning to start profiling people that you veer away from strangers. In order to really understand people you do not know, you will have to observe them for a period of time. This is why choosing a significant other, friend or co-worker is best to get your feet wet.

It is crucial to understand and recognize the "baseline profile" of the person you will be practicing on. This state is when the person is the most comfortable or at ease. Then, you can move on to observing their behaviors at random times. It may be a good idea to have a notebook with you at first, to jot down how the person you are observing behaves during different activities, days and how they interact with others.

Once you have gathered enough notes over a period of time of observation, you can now start to shape a list of patterns and common traits from the person's actions. Doing this creates a foundation to start building the truth of that person.

- Body language

- Facial expressions

- Eye movements

- Varying vocal tones

Then, it is time to jot out a list of unexpected behaviors, moments and other ticks that do not seem to fit into the "baseline" profile of the person you are observing.

Enhancing Your Knowledge

Now that you have gained some practice, it is time to profile someone you do not know or someone you wish to know better.

Define who they are – Allow their styles, appearance, and personality come out to "become them."

Recognize their vocalization towards a variety of people – Those that have a soft tone in their voice might signify that they are shy individuals, but you must also take note of the environment in which they are placed in as well. Louder tones of voice may signal that they feel the need to feel "higher" than those around them or like to be in command and in charge of other people. Does their voice change when defending an opinion? Do they communicate in an immature or mature way? Ensure that you are doing a good job of deciphering between conversational exaggerations, slang, sarcasm, etc. Pay attention to the context of words and how that person allows them to flow as they talk as well.

Take notice of their personal space – Compare how they represent themselves in a public setting like work compared to how they present themselves in a comfortable, home environment.

- What type of neighborhood do they reside in? Lower income housing may portray that they can afford to live in their means, with a bit of help or if in a wealthy area, they make more money than the average person.

- How are their organizational skills? Do not be too quick to come to a conclusion on this one. Perhaps their life is a bit unorganized because of the simple fact that they do not have time to keep it kept up and clean. Organized people typically show these skills in a public setting, are more confident and are less stressful than those that are disorganized.

- How do they choose to share their personal life with other people? Offices at work are places of comfort at the workplace, at least most of the time. Many workers hang photos of family and friends on the walls or on their desks. These little details can tell you a lot about a person's personal life in itself.

Take a Look at their Fashion Choices

You should view fashion judgments as you would homes and vehicles. It is easy to see how organized a person's life is by the way they dress and present themselves every day.

- Tucked in, casual or loose? Clothed for business or casual vacation? Professional, fitted or someone that lives perhaps in the outskirts?

- Hairstyle? Does it look as if they spent a lot of time of their hair or does it look like they didn't take as much time? Simple or complex style? The "look and go" people may live along with the concept if it looks good enough, they are seen as doing the best they can for the public eye.

- Footwear? Does it look as if they have their shoes shined frequently or do they look like the more "wear and tear" kind of individual?

View Reactions to Sudden Occurrences in Public

If they burp, do they make a move to conceal the noise? Coughing, sneezing and burping in various ways can be a way to separate those from whom who have proper etiquette.

Look at Eye Movements

Does the person you are observing tend to look straight into the eyes of others or off to the side or down to the ground? Do their eyes stray away when they are asked to provide an honest answer?

Evaluate their Self-Composure

Many people tend to be nervous when put into crowded areas and like to think of ways they can avoid going or being there. Those that are impatient in nature tap their feet more than calm people. Look for fidgeting, such as sighing, looking at their phone or watch lip biting as well.

Red Flags to Look For

To read people in an utmost and accurate manner, one must be willing to venture beyond the superficial traits and observations of certain behaviors. The following are some red flags to be aware of while in the midst of analyzing people.

- **Anger easily or like to talk about violence** – Those who have a short fuse in one particular situation is more than likely going to have one again in another situation, no matter what it is. For example, if the person you are observing road rage, this may indicate that they have anger issues outside of the car as well. Also, if they think that violence is a good answer and solves issues to many things they discuss, this is a red flag.

- **Physically aggressive and/or abusive to other people** – Had the individual you are analyzing ever been highly aggressive towards other people? How do they tend to treat servers/waiters at a restaurant? If they tend to lean towards mistreatment of bullying other people, this more than likely spills over into other parts of their lives as well.

- **They tend to place blame on everyone but themselves** – If while analyzing someone the topic of past relationships come up, and they mention that everything in relationships has been the other person's fault, it might not be a surprise that their current or future relationships, both friendship and otherwise, may not last long.

- **Lack of compassion for other people** – A lack of empathy and compassion for other people indicates that that person's character may not be as polished as they make it seem on the outside. They may lead towards more dangerous things. Experienced analyzers can typically pick up a person's level of empathy for other individuals in a matter of a 10-minute simple conversation. Those that lack empathy tend to take away the conversation, interrupting and attempting to refocus it on another subject.

Chapter 7
Tips and Tricks to Become a Better Analyzer

The best part of becoming an analyzer is that you do not have to go to a fancy FBI school in order to get into the minds of what people are thinking and feeling. People give off signals all the time, we just are typically blind to them unless we take the time to become educated on the tiniest of movements. It is all about knowing just what to look for in order to come to a conclusion about someone and crack their code. While there are no surefire methods to decipher what someone may be thinking, here are some awesome tips and tricks to help you in your future analyzing adventures!

- Begin with baseline reading. This will help you to establish a person's little quirks and so forth. A common way to do this is to give yourself time to observe a person's habits. This takes patience because some people are pretty hard to read. Even if you think a habit is not worth noting, note it anyways. Once you look back at your notes, even the little movements, habits or other actions that person took that seemed unessential at the time can pull many other notes you have jotted down together.

- Did you know that the question of "how are you doing today?" could be a question that someone else is using to probe you in order to decipher your baseline? Salespeople utilize this tactic quite frequently in order to read your baseline and get your set up for inquiries that involve more questions to get you to purchase something they are selling.

- Be aware of inconsistencies in a person's baseline personality versus gestures, words, and actions that do not quite fit in. This will help you to shape an overall personality profile over time.

- Ask specific, not vague questions. Open-ended inquiries do not work in truly reading anyone. Vague questions offer an opportunity to ramble in order for them to answer it, which makes it much more difficult to detect any sort of dishonesty. Ask questions that require people to provide you with a straight answer, but do not be too intrusive. Simple ask away, sit back and observe without interruption. This is where you will find that you receive your best inside information on this specific person.

- As you have learned, always be weary of a person's choice of words. They provide great insight as what a person is really trying to convey.

- Pay attention how a person leans. If their torso is facing away from you, this may indicate that this person is feeling stressed. It can also mean that they have much more on their mind than what you are attempting to say to soak into their minds.

- Gestures, like rubbing of the palms, touching and/or rubbing the forehead or rubbing palms against one's thigh highly, indicates that this individual is feeling rather stressed.

- Never underestimate facial cues. Watch for furrowing of the brow, tightening of the neck and facial muscles, clenching of the jaw and lip compressions. These are all signs of discomfort and distress.

- Watch how people tend to stall. If you are observing and notice someone that closes their eyes longer than it takes for a simple blink, take the time to clear their throat or asks you to repeat questions or what you have verbalized, they are taking the time to stall to avoid something.

- Excessive blinking, fidgeting and a lack of eye contact are all tell-tale signs that someone is lying. However, these can be precursors to someone who may feel anxious about a situation as well. It is common for those that are lying through their teeth to look at those they speak with straight in the eyes. This can also signify that they are attempting to deceit you.

- Other depictions of someone being dishonest are the utilization of vagueness in extremely descriptive formats or a quivering voice.

- Especially in women, if you are to observe them touching the area in the middle frontal part of their neck this may mean they are "protecting" themselves, which can be a signal of being uncomfortable.

- On the contrary, men typically will stroke their necks when in discomforting scenarios in an attempt to lower their heart rate.

- Eyes are not only a window to the soul. Excessive squinting and the constriction of the pupils may mean that this person may be bothered by what they are viewing.

- Utilization of cathartic exhales, known as highly audible and long exhales, indicates that a person is under extreme emotional distress. They will more than likely use frequent movements as well, such as rapid hand gestures. These actions are typically seen just moments right before and after they have been caught doing something they were not supposed to be.

- To improve detection of lies, take the time to observe children and how they act when they tell a white lie. We as adults typically learn to tell white lies in order to survive in social environments but children have yet to learn this prominent skill. They are bad at being dishonest, which gives those that are practicing their beginning analyzing skills a great place to start observing actions when lying. One must keep in mind that some adults are much better at lying than others. Those that are not so good at it will show similar signs to that of dishonest children.

- Learning how to read people takes time and experience. A "crash course" may get you on a good path to stardom but it will not cut it when reading people really counts. In order to get better at honing these types of skills, practice makes perfect. And you must constantly practice these skills in order to keep them fresh in your mind and keep your mind to viewing them sharp. While there are classes and online training courses you can take to learn more, do not think you are an expert after printing off a certificate of completion. Real experts develop the skill constantly by observing and listening in the midst of everyday life.

- To become a better analyzer, it is especially important at the beginning stages to get some sort of feedback on how accurate you are. If you do not do this, you will never truly know if you are improving your reading skills or not.

- In order to get to know people faster, analyzers must be willing to start with the boring facts first in order to build a foundation to really profile a person. Factual Inquiries are easy for anyone to answer. In order to hone your analyzing skills, you must be willing to observe and listen closely and remain a curious individual. You may come across quite a few intriguing stories as to how people got to where they are today!

  - Where did you grow up?

  - What do you do for fun?

  - How long have you worked where you are now?

  - Interests? Hobbies?

  - Where was your first job?

  - Etc, etc.

- Learn the motive of an individual. If the building of a good rapport is finally going well, it is time to begin asking causative inquiries. These are what will help you dive deeper into the person, why they make the decisions they do, what motivates them, etc. While there is absolutely nothing wrong with just flat out asking what drives a person, you will get more detailed answers if you are specific questions related to the topic.

  - Why did you pick that particular college?

  - What caused you to become interested in____?

  - What made you pursue your profession?

  - How did you come across the organization you work for?

  - How did you become involved in this hobby?

  - Etc, etc. By the way, do not be afraid to be creative in the questions you form to ask. People appreciate it!

- Reveal the worth of the things that make up the person's life – Everyone has different sets of values for different things in their life. So everyone has values in some form or another. But it can be hard to get a good answer from this type of inquiry when it comes to analyzing that person's personality. Simply asking what their values are can tend to be awkward. It is important to build a rapport with this person before you start diving into these types of questions. Here are some to give you an idea:

- What person had the most impact on you in your life so far?

- If you had the chance to do it all over again, what would you do differently?

- Looking back over your career and work life, what was a major turning point that you can recall?

- What are the high points that are memorable in your life?

- What words of wisdom would you give to your younger self or a young person in your life if they came to you for advice?

Chapter 8
Why Do People Do the Things They Do?

The Variety in Motivation

One of the crucial premises of the Act of Nonviolent Communication is that everything any of us ever does is an endeavor to meet central human needs. Much can be stated, and I have expounded on it sometime recently, about what precisely considers a need, and the distinction amongst needs and the numerous procedures we utilize in our endeavors to meet them. There is no claim inside this training we are all the same; just that we share a similar central needs, and they fill in as the main purpose for us to do anything.

On the off chance that everything is roused by at least one human need, at that point why am I notwithstanding discussing assortments of inspirations? This is on the grounds that what fluctuates is the level of mindfulness we convey to the connection between our requirements and our activities. To the extent I can advise in view of my presentation to various societies, our different societies don't, for the most part, develop in us the act of recognizing what we need. In actuality, quite a bit of socialization is centered around addressing what we need and disclosing to us any number of explanations behind acting other than in light of the fact that we need something. This, to me, is a disaster of gigantic extents, since what at that point happens is that what we need goes underground: we keep on acting in view of our needs without realizing what they are, and consequently with far less decision than we may some way or another do.

When we don't know about necessities, we act in view of our emotions, contemplations, propensities, or drive. Basically, each of these sorts of inspiration can fill in as an approach to deny our duty regarding our decisions. Albeit each of these are associated with our necessities, unless we particularly connect with the fundamental needs, we are probably going to keep on acting with less decision than we can develop and accomplish through getting to be require educated.

Feelings and Thoughts

Unless we build up some sort of routine with regards to cognizant engagement with our emotions, the greater part of us encounter them and react to them as inward requests for activity or evasion of activity regardless of whether it's what we need. Dread, disgrace, or blame may lead us to evasion, while outrage or energy drives us to move towards an activity.

When we in a flash make an interpretation of sentiments into activities, we avoid any comprehension of what we really need. As a result of the quality of which our emotions "charge" activity, we don't have the chance to utilize sentiments as what I trust they are intended for, which is to be wellsprings of data. Emotions, I come to comprehend them in view of perusing, self-examination, and working with others, serve a flag work. They emerge from the consistent stream of information about what is going on, and our incessant assessment, under the radar of our mindfulness, with reference to regardless of whether our necessities are met. Tuning into our sentiments painstakingly enables us to follow them to the hidden needs that offer ascent to them. The decision lies unequivocally there, in the ability to comprehend, get to, and grasp the basic needs.

There are many practices that help nearness, most eminently assortments of contemplation. However far we get with such practices, they don't consequently give access to knowing our needs. Without a solid routine with regards to pointing our consideration on distinguishing needs, we are much more inclined to interface our sentiments to musings, which are as yet expelled from what I see as our essential, innate inspiration.

Considerations cover our decision uniquely in contrast to our emotions. When we act in view of what we ought to do, must do, or need to do, what we can't do, what others will state, what is "objective and sensible" or "proper," we are connecting our activities to something that is generally outer to us. Sentiments propel us from inside, while contemplations urge us from outside. The reason this is of such essential significance to me is on account of flexibility is about picking as opposed to being constrained. The decision is constantly inside us: we may, and regularly will, mull over the impact of our activities and decisions on others. All things considered, there is a significant improvement between trusting we need to accomplish something, and picking it in light of what's essential to us underneath the "need to".

Habits

While sentiments and considerations give us the figment of a decision, propensities are perceived by the greater part of us as lacking decision. Therefore, when individuals start the act of figuring out how to interfere with their requirements, they effortlessly fall into judging their propensities. I can't envision that any positive change can rise up out of self-judgment instead of from understanding the necessities of the propensities plan to serve and discovering decision in how to take care of them.

Some portion of the trouble with changing propensities into the decision is that we frequently are not by any means mindful of making a move in view of a propensity. It's just at different circumstances, far from the activity, that we may wind up noticeably mindful that we acted in view of a propensity. Those are likewise the circumstances we are destined to judge ourselves for the chronic conduct. Makes it considerably all the more difficult that finding the necessities that offer ascent to the propensity requires profound sleuthing, in light of the fact that the propensities were shaped before, when particular activities may have been capable methodologies to address certain issues, and those extremely same systems may never again take care of those necessities. Propensities, by their tendency, are intended to calm us from choosing newly each time, so it's not liable to be anything but difficult to recover decision. Thus, sympathy for self is basic. It's just when we have adequate delicacy towards how hard changing propensities can be that we can make an alternate inspiration for the procedure of progress itself: rather than being roused by "should" considering, we can discover the necessities that lead us to need to draw in with the propensity. Regularly, for me, these are opportunity and legitimacy, which are intense helpers. They might possibly be the same for other people who are perusing this. Grasping every one of our needs in connection to our propensities may move the enthusiastic nature of attempting to roll out an improvement, for instance, from criticalness to quiet resolve. This establishing can enable us to grieve any neglected needs that the propensities prompt, imagine different procedures to meet the greatest number of necessities as we can, and grow clear demands of ourselves to help the coveted change.

I can't sufficiently stretch that it is so basic to achieve full association with the necessities that lead us to pick the routine conduct. This association is basic for rolling out the improvement that is grounded in self-empathy. Without this quality, we can't have adequate inside participation, and the endeavor to change is probably going to be a self-request that will reproduce inward imperviousness to the change.

Impulse and Intuition

The last contender I am mindful of for being an essential help is motivation. Like propensities, driving forces are perceived as lacking decision and are in this manner judged. In opposition to propensities, however, motivations show up as "normal" and brimming with life. Now and again, particularly when we have been oppressed by propensities and excruciating idea designs, reacting to our driving forces and following up on them can appear like an appreciated alleviation. They can give us the deception of returning to ourselves.

I was helped by a discussion with an insightful companion who said that he never utilizes the class "characteristic." We have been raised, for such a variety of centuries, in ways that control and change whatever our "tendency" is, that none of us can genuinely recognize what is or isn't common. Rather, he makes a qualification between what is unconstrained and what is thinking. What he calls thinking is the thing that I allude to as cognizant decision.

Unmistakably, driving forces are totally unconstrained, but then they may not really be identified with what we genuinely need. Our driving forces can emerge for such a large number of reasons, and without anyone else, we have no unmistakable approach to evaluate their ability to satisfy needs.

Rather, I have been expecting to build up an inward ability to recognize motivation from instinct. I wish I could put this distinction into clear and learnable strides. All I know to state is that instinct appears to originate from an alternate inner place, and doesn't have the constraint or the drive. Mine has a tendency to be delicate and clear. Simply seeing it gives some inward association, some discharge, and clearness. A drive, similar to an inclination, has a nature of moving us to action. I don't have a comparable involvement with instinct. Regularly, its voice is delicate and requires watchful consideration regarding perceiving what is being said. For myself, I respect and appreciate my instinct, remembering it as a wellspring of knowledge, an immediate access to what I need without the careful exertion of observing what my necessities are.

Conclusion

Thank you for making it through to the end of *How to Analyze People*.

I hope that the contents of this book were able to adequately provide you with detailed insight into the actions, speech, and body language of those around you and how learning about various personality types can aid you in getting a couple steps ahead of other like-minded individuals.

I hope that the information you have newly acquired was able to provide you with all the tips, tricks, and tools you need to successfully get started in learning how to analyze those in your everyday life as well as strangers you come across. I hope that the knowledge you have absorbed makes you more than capable of achieving your goals of getting to know people for who they really are rather than who they are just attempting to be.

The next step is to put the information and the tips that you have within your hand to the test! Start small, working your way through family and friends until you get the hang of analyzing techniques. Be patient with yourself, for practice makes perfect! Soon, you will be the one people turn to for answers about those in their life! Good luck in all the newly found knowledge you will gain through the techniques you have acquired from this book!

www.ingramcontent.com/pod-product-compliance
Lightning Source LLC
Chambersburg PA
CBHW071237280526
45787CB00002B/965